THE BRUMBACK LIBRARY

OF VAN WERT COUNTY

VAN WERT, OHIO

The Collected Poems of Beatrice Hawley

6/30/89

THE
Collected
Poems
OF
Beatrice
Hawley

Edited & with
an Introduction by
DENISE LEVERTOV

ZOLAND BOOKS, INC.
Cambridge, Massachusetts

vw $S BT Vwm √CA

First edition published in 1989 by
Zoland Books, Inc.
P.O. Box 2766
Cambridge, Massachusetts 02238

Library of Congress Catalog Card Number: 89-050430
ISBN 0-944072-08-9
ISBN 0-944072-09-7 (soft)

FIRST EDITION
Printed in the United States of America

Zoland Books extends a special thank you to Ed Hogan and
Hugh Abernethy of Zephyr Press; for referring the manu-
script to us, and for promoting Beatrice Hawley's work.

The poems originally appearing in Making the House Fall
Down (Alice James Books, 1977) and Nothing is Lost
(Applewood Books, 1979) are reprinted with the permission
of the publishers. Poems from the third book have recently
appeared in the following journals: The American Poetry
Review, The Atlantic, Iowa Review, Kalliope, Mid-
American Review, RE:AL and Seneca Review.

Contents

v

➤ᴣ *Nothing Is Lost*

❧ The Third Book (Uncollected Poems)

viii

Introduction

When Beatrice Hawley was alive I knew her as a friend whose kindness and generosity were a touchstone; as an admired activist for peace and justice; and as a lyrical and original talent. To have been chosen from among her many poet friends to edit the work she left unpublished at the time of her death has been a privilege bringing with it both joy and sadness. Joy at the power and delicacy so uniquely blended in these poems; sorrow not only because she was a loved presence now missing, her absence become a part of life's texture, but because in surveying her work I have been aware of not having fully realized how much she had achieved until it was too late to tell her of that recognition. Though she was one of the least conceited of people, I believe she did have a sense of her own worth, of the quality of her own gift; but every artist enjoys, and sometimes needs, the acclaim of fellow-members of the tribe — an acclaim which unfortunately often does not mature until after his or her death.

Bea's poetry was known and appreciated (chiefly in the Boston area where both the books published during her lifetime appeared,[1] and where she often read) but she had not established a major, national reputation. The clearer recognition of Beatrice's achievement to which I have come is due partly to the close attention demanded by the task of arranging the poems, collating different versions and so on; but it is also the result of seeing the unpublished work in juxtaposition with the two earlier books — thus it is an experience other readers will share. Viewing her poetic work as a totality it is possible to see recurrent themes which appear in both the published and unpublished poems and to hear her voice more distinctly.

With this in mind, I have not followed a chronological sequence in arranging the unpublished poems (indeed, even if I had wished to, it would have been conjectural at best,

[1] *Making the House Fall Down* (Alice James Books, 1977); *Nothing Is Lost* (Applewood Books, 1979).

based only on the return address given in some instances or on the condition of the sheet of paper in others, and only rarely on an internal reference or an actual date). Instead, I have followed a practice developed in assembling my own books, that of dividing contents into titled sections (while leaving the published collections unchanged, of course). In assigning poems to these thematic categories I have acted alone; only I am to blame for whatever may be felt to be a misreading of the gist of this or that poem. Beatrice herself might not have agreed with the section titles; are some poems, grouped as Joy, really Griefs? Are some Griefs Joys? One thing is certain: she would fully have understood the intent, and forgiven lapses in its execution. Knowing that — because that is what it was to know *her* — I have been emboldened to proceed.

Beatrice, as the daughter of a member of the U.S. Consular service, spent much of her childhood abroad and was exposed from infancy to other cultures and other languages. The greater part of her early years was spent in Italy, but she and her younger sister were sent to French *lycées* there. There were also periods of residence in the U.S., mainly in Connecticut where her grandparents lived; she graduated from high school in Old Saybrook, Connecticut. She loved Italy passionately; loved it despite a brief stay in a pediatric sanatorium (she and her two younger sisters having come down with TB, the middle sister very seriously) which brought her to an unusually early awareness of death (she was only five or six at the time, but knew that "the nuns tell lies/'Maria has gone to live with the angels'"); and despite a profound sense of loneliness in childhood, which grew even sharper during her adolescence, as she recounts in a number of unpublished prose writings. In 1970, when, after her divorce and the death of an infant daughter, she had made a return visit to Italy as to a place of refuge, she wrote to a friend, "That's the whole trouble with us. We haven't got our country. When I'm here I long for there. When I'm there I long for here. Here's what I wrote this morning..."[2]

[2] Bilingual in the original.

Devo trovare la mia patria di nuovo	I must find my homeland again
La patria di marmo dove sogniai	The marble homeland where I dreamed
Tutti piccoli sogni dorati di gioventu	All the little young golden dreams
Tutti momenti in attesa, aspetando la mia vita	All the waiting moments, waiting for my life.
L'ho perduta, non e piu mia	I have lost her, she is not mine
Qui fa sempre freddo, questa e fatta	This one is cold and all made of
Tutta di legno, tutta di machine, e questa	Wood and machines and this one
E veramente la mia, freddo nel mio sangue	Is really mine, cold is in my blood.
Sono la bimba del Nord, che mi	I am the child of the North, which they
Chiamavano nella vita d'oro perduto	Called me in my lost gold life
Piccola sempre, occhi celesti, manine nervose	Forever small, eyes blue, small nervous hands,
Pien di paura d'aver sempre perduto il mio sole	Filled with the fear of having forever lost my sun.

"I love to write in Italian and French and English," she continued, "because they are all so different. You can really write that way in Italian, it is awful in English...." Again, in a prose piece recalling the garden at Bellosguardo near Florence where several years of her childhood were spent, "a stone house with a tower & a garden, right next door to Henry James's," she wrote:

> I myself have sat in an almond tree while the almonds were still green, and eaten through that green...the greenest

thing I have ever done....I wont even start on the olive groves. Olive groves! Bent, grey, dark, low, perfect, peace, heavy trunks. That's all I can say about that. You make up the rest. It wont be easy....The very dust is golden. The stones themselves are rich and heavy. A child cannot see the ceiling. Every winter the lemons, oranges & jasmine are put in the witch's wing called a limonaia. Summer they come around the back staircase again. A child is too small to see over the edges of the large pottery pots. She likes them when they moisten and smell. Medium is not possible there. It's never ordinary. Heat, cold. One day walking along the paths of a garden you are transformed by joy, the next by terror.... Peach tree and peas on the lower level. No little boy to steal them, or the oranges, or the lemons, or a sprig of jasmine. The walls are far too high, matted solid with ivy. All around the walls, out there, the fields sloping down from the hill. That earth is also rich and smells more brown, more red. Many times those fields must have been soaked with blood, enriched. But there has never been a metal battle there. Just the old kind, when the losers just lie looking at the sky above, and bleed to death.

The passage goes on to speak of modern bomb warfare, of "pacification" and the desolate landscapes left after it.

"But that's a 20th c digression," she adds, "...the likelihood of those Bellosguardo fields being pacified is very slender. The garden grows, and the marguerites."

But though Beatrice loved Italy, she also suffered there. As the eldest sister her sense of responsibility developed early, especially as their parents travelled a lot and the children were in the care of maids. And when the family, after a couple of years in Connecticut, moved to Arlington, Virginia, Beatrice "hated it," one of her sisters has told me:

She was always a champion of the underdog & there were so many little Black and Jewish kids who were victims. Bibi befriended them and fought (usually physically though she was the smallest girl in the class) their oppressors.

By the time they moved back to Italy (to Rome) the girls had forgotten their Italian. They were sent to the French *lycée*.

"B. was around 14 & suffered from the transplantation,"
says her sister.

> She was a unique character in a terribly conformist school
> and world. She was in the throes of adolescence (and I
> think throes is the operative word). I remember that she
> started smoking then & she used to sit in her room which
> was very dark (she used to close her shutters to make it
> darker) and festooned with a large dark brown fishing net.
> She had a record of Garcia Lorca poems & she played it and
> read Lorca over & over.

The next change of residence was to Trieste, where "it was
still worse for an adolescent" as the sisters were not in
school but had a tutor and correspondence lessons, an
isolation which, unrealized by adults, intensified the feelings
of acute loneliness, of being different from others, and
afraid — feelings common to many teenagers but unusually
acute in Beatrice at that time and during several later times
in her life.

She had in fact more than her fair share of trouble and
suffering during her forty-one years of life. She was thrice
married, twice divorced; her loving third marriage was beset
with economic difficulties. Her first child, a son, lived to
give her much delight, but the second and third — both
daughters — died in early infancy. Her academic career,
started late because of her early first marriage, was successful,
but was interrupted by illness before she could obtain her
PhD. Often poor, she cooked, catered, and sewed for a living
at various times. And all her life she struggled with ill
health: the TB in childhood; several hospitalizations (starting
in her teens) for emotional breakdowns; and later on, systemic
lupus with all its attendant problems such as joint pains and
kidney malfunction, plus its treatment by steroids, which
have severe side effects; and finally the cancer which killed
her. But she *did* struggle. Fragments of diaries about her
mental breakdowns (all of which took place before I knew
her, that is to say before the last decade of her life) reveal how
much the will to live coexisted with her intense awareness

of death as an evil force, a presence, which held her captive in overwhelming loneliness at times but against which — or whom — she fought earnestly, and won. And was again attacked — and won again. Many times.

As I knew her she was indeed a woman of great strength, a hard-earned strength and tenderheartedness in the midst of physical weakness and of all the moral suffering of one unremittingly aware of the oppressions and horrors of our time. Few of her poems are directly "engaged," just as few of them are autobiographically "confessional" in any blatant manner; one could not derive much information about her private history from them, nor do they take on the task of relating or directly addressing public history. But Beatrice was a leading spirit and persistent worker for many causes and organizations: for example, for several years she counselled young parents in behalf of the Boston Association for Childbirth Education, of which she was Vice President and editor of the newsletter; she was a founding member of Common Stock Restaurant, a worker-owned collective which served as a forum for many political groups (here she worked at everything from cooking to dishwashing, bookkeeping to internal wall-construction); was an organizer of the Boston Bail Fund (and also the Ella Ellison Defense Committee which secured a new trial and a verdict of innocent for this Black defendant); worked with and for the American Friends Service Committee on various peace projects[3]; was an active member of the Alice James publishing collective; founded New England Writers for Survival to mobilize writers to use their professional skills and connections in the service of peace and disarmament.... These are just a few of her activities; and I am sure many of

[3] Among these was a week's participation in the Tiger Cage Project on the steps of the Capitol in 1974, which demonstrated what these cages were like, where prisoners were being kept by the vicious, though crumbling, U.S.-supported Thieu and Lon Nol regimes in Viet-Nam and Cambodia. Volunteers in the project, fasting, spent two or three hours a day each in the cage, shackled by the legs and crossed wrists, unable to stand or move. A prose piece of hers describes the experience vividly.

the people who knew her in those connections had no idea she was a poet; or if they did, it was accidentally learned, for she was far more of a listener, socially, than a talker. She could, however, be assertive when it was necessary; and though she did so much for causes and for individuals, she was no sentimentalist: "I know that many so-called 'movement' people operate by feeling guilty and making other people feel guilty..." she wrote to a friend, "but if there's one thing I really feel strongly it's that neither I nor anyone else has the 'answer,' the right way, the correct method, etc. And I can't categorize people. I can't like someone just because they're poor or black or a woman or whatever. I like the people I like and I don't like the people I don't like. I trust my feelings about that...about people."

And she was sometimes amused and taken aback at herself when the medication she was taking for lupus (before she found she also had cancer) made her outspokenly aggressive. "I should put this to some use," she would say; "John [her husband] thinks I should go down to the White House...." She wrote, "Psychologically, this...experience is providing me with some short cuts I hope I don't lose when I get better.... I called the librarian a fascist yesterday.... Thank God I found out later that's the way normal people usually react to him. Anyway," she continues, "on the positive side the nice thing is to be very focussed during the times when I am clearheaded. I've gotten not quite as nice and yessie as I used to be and quite picky about what I do with my time. The list of people I really, really love is not that long, after all. I've spent an awful lot of time worrying about being loved by just everyone who breathes. I even used to be nice to that librarian. I'm liking myself a lot more."

One of the sources of that ability to give to others, to strike her friends as a pillar of inner strength, was doubtless the very struggle she had endured with such severe insecurities. Another source, which remained unknown to many of her friends since she did not "talk it up," was her deep religious faith. She was a communicant in the Episcopal Church, and always kept close to her the copy of the Book of Common Prayer she had been given at her Confirmation. (It is typical of her that when my son was desperately ill in 1982 she pressed this treasured volume into my hands to help and comfort me.)

What were some of the literary influences on her poetry — and how can one characterize her own work? In some very early poems (not included here) ee cummings is easily detectable; somewhat later, Theodore Roethke; maybe Sylvia Plath, to whom she dedicated a poem (p. 69). In her mature work I see affinities, rather than influences. Mark Strand (with whom she studied one summer at Breadloaf, and later saw sometimes, and exchanged letters)[4] and W.S. Merwin might come to mind — but if there are occasional resemblances to their styles in Hawley, it surely results from the influence of, or affinity with, Emily Dickinson, from whom they possibly, and she certainly, drew much nourishment.

Dickinson, like cummings, is a poet too idiosyncratic to serve as a direct model; only naive high school students are unaware of how obvious it is who they have been reading when they use her as one. But a true natural affinity surely existed between Bea and Emily Dickinson. She shared with this poet (for whom it seems she had a special love which must have acknowledged that sharing)[5] an oblique and curious angle of vision (as if from the cocked head and bright eye of an observant robin) which contrasted with the level, unsurprising way of looking most of us have most of the time; and in both poets this gives to their diction its special nuances. It is a quality no one can imitate; and which is as hard to describe or analyze as a taste or a fragrance.

Hawley's poetry is delicately sensual in music and perception, but her interest, like Emily Dickinson's, is in the metaphysical significance of her images and not in simple description. She did not, however, lapse into abstractions; the concrete images vital to metaphor are never

---

[4] She also worked at Brandeis with Allen Grossman, for whom she had great respect and admiration. But I see no similarities between his work and hers.

[5] I have not been able to trace an essay she wrote on Emily Dickinson, but have been assured it was written.

wanting in her work, and the character of her daily life helped in this: a person who regularly, and of necessity, does physical work (and Bea continued to have to cook and clean and sew, both at home and for a living, throughout the years when she was in graduate school and teaching) has less time for creative work than is desirable, yet has the advantage of a grounding, a mine of objective correlatives, often missing in those who seem luckier in their privileged leisure or more intellectual labor. In Bea's case, her down-to-earth abilities wonderfully balanced an imagination which might otherwise have been too ethereal; and her poetry owes much to this balance.

In the later unpublished poems, there is some tendency for the metaphysical dimension to become more dominant; but by then the concrete and sensuous had so firmly established itself in her craft that this could occur without deleterious effect — on the contrary, it permitted her a new freedom of imagination, a still fuller expression of all that was wild and strange in her, an ethereality winged with honest-to-goodness feathers.

In January 1981 Beatrice wrote,

> Here is something that says more clearly how I feel about the way I'm trying to see life, live life:
> "...be patient toward all that is unsolved in your heart and try to love *the questions themselves*.... Do not now seek the answers, because you would not be able to live them. And the point is, to live everything. *Live* the questions now. Perhaps you will then gradually, without noticing it, live along some distant day into the answer. Perhaps you do carry within yourself the possibility of shaping and forming as a particularly happy and pure way of living; train yourself to it — but take whatever comes with great trust, and only if it comes out of your own will, out of some need of your inmost being, take it upon yourself and hate nothing."[6]
> What I am concerned with is precisely "that possibility of shaping & forming as a particularly happy & pure way

[6] From Rilke's *Letters to a Young Poet*.

of living." Working out the hope for a few good poems (if I am very lucky and very very attentive) is the major focus of my conscious and unconscious work-life. It is my particular good fortune to find myself housed and to be able to financially support this endeavor: and the style of living needs to be minimal for what I want to do. So even the leanest seeming moments are quite bounteous considering I have my morning hours in solitude.
And a wonderful wonderful son. And family life.

There is so much of Beatrice in that passage: the way she perceives as good fortune an economic status, and the resulting claims on her time and energies, many people would have constantly complained about; and the humble but unswerving commitment to poetry — humble, but simultaneously ambitious in the sense of desiring to create, to be the means of creating, true poems. Earlier (1976) she had written, "I'm not producing enough, or enough good. I've been scared to go to a couple of workshops I've been invited to join because I just don't feel I have enough good work to warrant it." But by the mid-eighties, though illness (and the treatments for it with their powerful and sometimes devastating side effects) cut down and eventually stopped her writing, I think — from my own impressions and from what others have told me — that she knew herself to be at least partially fulfilled as a poet. As late as August 1984 — eight months before her death — an entry in her journal read: "...poems, good and bad, are coming back with their insistence, forcing me to understand them well enough to give them some shape, some garment they can wear as they try, like little birds, to make their way in the world, apart from me. This is my job..."

Missing Beatrice

Goodness was
a fever in you. Anyone

might glow in the heat of it,
go home comforted —

for them a shawl, for you
fire at the bone.

•

You knew
more than was good for you.
Your innocence
was peat-bog water, subtle and dark,
that cold it was,
that pure.

•

Kindness — didn't we act as though
we could cut an endless supply from you
like turf from a bog?

•

Smoke of that empty hearth
fragrant still.
Your words
cupped in our hands to drink.
But you —
you're gone and we never
really saw you.

—Denise Levertov

Making the
House
Fall Down

This book is for S.E.

I

The Rag-Picker

The woman who walks along the streets
is the woman collecting rags.
They fly to her from windows:
flags, silks, bridal sheets.

She is taller than the gates,
tucks her elbows in to shout.
She bundles everything and takes
it all home to her hills.

At night she comes back wearing her cloak,
the magic rings tight against her cheeks
make her mouth bloody as she leans
over the beds of children asleep.

Psyche

Psyche, with her hair streaming, runs inside.
She's had a dream while sleeping in the meadow.
It must be done. She tries to hide.
There is no time. The sound of men below
swallows her. They have ropes, they'll push
her out to rocks, pin her for the sake of all
their daughters. Now the mountain is hushed.
The men steal away, eyes down. Night falls.
Psyche remembers her dolls, the pots she took
to play at house. This is where it leads. Asked
to accept a rapist, told she must not look.
In the end she loves him, but Eros is masked.
She lights a candle once to see her lover:
we are still looking for him with her.

The Painter

For the woman's body, use hills,
for the children, use bowls of fruit,
for the house, use lace on a round table.

You paint living in a house,
you are a woman with children who come to visit,
a woman who knows how to use hammer and nails.

For the lovers, paint flowers,
for music, paint the Spanish shawl,
for the mother, paint a bridge.

When the lights go out
and the walls are invisible
the landscapes and still lifes
speak to each other about the way
you love them without words;
they tell each other which person they hide.

The Potter

You get clay
red clay, from the potter
who hunches down
at the river's edge
near a large city.

He makes each pot perfect
he rolls them out to dry
under the sun. They bake.

After the river dries
the city moves to another delta.

The clay becomes motes of dust
dancing in your room
when you are a little girl
waking up from your nap.

You figure this out,
grown woman with clay
dusting your hair red.

The Travel Artist

Your thinning hair
wreathed in flowers, you
want a white house
near blue water.

Your family, a collection
of rich people, wave you
over oceans to settle
you down to earth.

You write letters to them:
"fire, fire, fire, fire,
my mail is censored the chief
of police is looking this way."

At night you shudder in your
new bed, you spill wine over
the sheets, you pull them
up to your chin.

Nightwalking

You wear your skirt
like a flag you are
using to keep the lions back.

Little traps of thread
form like birds behind you.

You walk as if
you could dance on water.

Your angel shrugs down feathers
to cover the stars in your hair.

All over town mothers of men
are crying when you go by.

The Elect

His hand can shatter
as much as a cow
standing in green crystal.

His voice can speak
and teapots pour out
alone to fill a ravine.

His hair is flutes,
the better mayor.
His following tuck
chickens under their arms.

The Cleaning Lady Thinks of Lizzie Borden

In summer it gets hot.
The cleaning lady thinks of Lizzie Borden.
She carries clothes to hang on the line;
she knows air and sun will dry them better.

The house behind her has many rooms.
She has cleaned them each in turn.
There is a barn here too, and a pear tree;
but there is no axe and the pears rot.

She hangs the boy's jeans.
She hangs the father's shirt.
She hangs the mother's nightgown.
Her arms ache.

The people who live in this house are not her parents.
The boy makes lemonade for her,
at the end of the day she gets money;
no one here wills her the slightest harm.

The cleaning lady has heard
that Lizzie, awaiting trial, day after day
would squeeze an egg — which would not break:
the matron told the story to the court.

In the hot kitchen the glass of lemonade
waits on the clean table. The cleaning lady
touches the cold beads to her cheek,
she knows if she tried to squeeze an egg, it would break.

Rules for the Cleaning Lady

Brush the twigs out of your hair if you live in a cave.
Enter quietly.
Love the animals in the house.
Don't feed the fish.
Never drink anything but one can of Diet Cola.
Eat one tuna salad sandwich on bread, not toast.
Ask for more vacuum cleaner bags.
If you bring a book hide it under a towel in the bathroom.
Read nowhere else.
Sit nowhere else.
Leave quietly.

You will be rewarded in heaven
where angels are even now weaving tapestries
to line the walls of your cave.

At the Clinic

We are still.
We look very much the same
as we did a week ago.
The weight in our bodies
is only the weight of a small stone.
Today we will hold
our hands together;
our eyes will hook
into each other:
we will rub each other's backs
and draw our knees up
under our chins.

On the way home on the same bus
our eyes will unlock.
These days teach us
how to be fierce, how to hold
on to ourselves.

Venice, 1949

The houses are sinking
no faster than before.
Beautiful women are still
buying gold, wearing it
on their arms.
She sells her rings, like the others.
Her daughters are in the country,
they are in the laps of nuns,
they are eating white grapes, they are dying.

But she is better off
than the Princess of Estonia,
who sleeps next door
in her shiny black dress,
all the emeralds gone.
She has a passport, she can travel,
she can buy medicine,
she can go to Philadelphia.
Her daughters will be cured,
she will buy them snowsuits.

II

Eclipse

A boy limping across a field,
to a barn of darkening cracks;
flowers closed at noon.

Under the house
animals are hidden:
clustered, organized, terrible.

Dream Poem

KATE dreams a fish,
its tail wound down her back;
the shawl her mother made
over and over one whole summer.

JOHN dreams a hole:
water, well, mirror,
his white hand reaches his white hand —
O! He is a boy. His father is laughing.

BEATRICE dreams a little boat,
the little boat of children who drown
one after another, she can see
the stars in their hair.

These dreamers row
into the dreams they sleep
in the same house,
they will be tied past morning.

Moving

We are getting ready to move
to a place near water:
small boats with lanterns,
prows up-turned, spearfishing.
The moon is continuous here,
houses made of lava,
fish drying in moonlight:
silver flakes on the path.

Beyond the antipodes
where light bends
and you can see it
my room has walls of blue chalk,
my floor is brown paper.
People lie on the paper
making outlines of angels:
each person makes a different angel
each angel covers a different person
even small children
are angel-covered.

There are peaches here,
there is jam to eat in winter
with tinned milk when it rains.
It is not far:
grandmothers may come and visit,
cousins can find work,
children learn the language quickly.
We are all going soon,
we will arrive early;
it will be morning
we will rub our eyes
we will see, see the land rise.

White Tents

Children in foreign countries
sleep under white tents
in summer.

Windows are left open,
voices come from the garden,
the voices of ghosts
who speak another language.

By day, during naps,
the country beyond the bed
is golden and the voices
more quiet than at night.

The mothers and fathers
do not know as they pull
the netting shut that the children,
safe from malaria,
are haunted.
They tell the children a story
of how the pots and pans in the kitchen
have dances at midnight.
When they leave the room
the children wait quietly
under the tents of mist
for the flowers and trees in the garden,
so much more alive,
to finally steal them.

The Ship

They are too high to see their eyes in the water.
The deck is a plain, and in the inner dining hall
the children are at table to eat more cake than
    they have seen.

The sea is darker than the ship above it.
The children's parents are walking about,
arms around each other like the old days
    before the journey.

This is the ship that takes the family home,
rocking them in her great belly as she moves
so surely to the other side of the water where
    they will land.

The Lovers

Be patient. They were young together:
she with her lawn-party hat,
he with his tennis-playing sweater.

They've been together for years.
It would take too long
to tear up the bedspread she made
loving every stitch of the way.

If there is a stain on it now,
he's been blind to it for centuries.
In the morning they find
each other under it,
their bones tangled together.

Evening

The inside of the shell
is our mother's room.
Into this room
our father comes at night
taking the coins
out of his pocket.

In the next room
my sisters and I are sleeping.
We take turns
waking in very dark
to hear the steady breathing;
without us it would stop.

Around the house
the moon pulls up the
seeds our mother planted.
All day my sisters and I
will weed her garden.
When our father comes home
the day will be over again.

The Lemon-House

In a garden full of ghosts
threads hang from the almond tree.
You are a child here
with a new place to hide every day.

The pots which hold the lemon trees
are bigger than you.
In winter they are wheeled into the lemon-house
where dry leaves pile
under the chimney.

You hide there one night:
the grown-ups are having a party.
In the morning your father finds you
and without speaking cradles you
and takes the twigs out of your hair
one by one.

Small Stones

Our mother lies on her throne of cushions,
we climb up to her room
on a dangerous ledge.
We carry them in our mouths,
keeping the balance;
our hands make marks on the sill.
We take turns bringing
small stones for her eyes.

The First Mother

Your arms pulled down the sky.
I was just
a high-strung child to mind:
a fingernail, a pale moon,
a white shell,
my thin skin
stretched tight over the pulse.

You set me down near stones and water,
taught the crayfish how to move
and me how to hold still.

You were a mountain,
picking me up with one arm.
All the way home
I could feel your secrets
rolling against my knees.

Eggs

My mother
puts many eggs in her food,
eggs are gold and silver to her,
they are treasures, they make
people see in the dark,
they make you smart in school.

I learn to swallow the yolk,
whole, to hold my breath,
to slide it down my throat.
All day I feel the knot
in my chest. I am not smart
in school. At night I am blind.

Hiding

I hide in the almond tree.
I am watching my mother
moving around the garden
with her silver scissors,
cutting flowers. She does
not see me. I see the glint
from the blades even when
my eyes are closed.

Nocturne

My sisters are writing at the kitchen table.
My father is washing my mother's hair.
I am upstairs looking out the window.
The salt marsh darkens.
I fill my bed with animals.

Spy

I am early.
No one is home.
When I am alone in the house
I do not know who I am.

I go upstairs.
I look in my mother's top drawer:
the nylon stockings are rolled up.
The scarves are folded.
Under the paper that lines the drawer
there is only wood.

Stolen Poem

I used to climb out of the back window,
I used to walk towards the marsh out back;
I used to walk towards the salt smell.
My shoes used to fill with water.
I used to get cold.

I used to do this at night,
I used to bless the sleeping house
in summer more than winter. I used to
fill my mouth with pennies;
I used to do this quietly.

I used to come back cold and smelly.
I used to steal back into the house.
The animals used to stay asleep,
The sleepers would not turn in their beds.

Mountains

Though I stand on mountains
I cannot find my body.
She is washed down by water,
she is missing.
From a long way up
there is no sign,
no red jacket,
no hair making its own rivers.

I have been looking for weeks in these hills.
No one has seen a sign of her.
Not for years on years.
Without my body
I am only light
breaking nothing.

Snapshot

My young mother stands
at the top of the stairs.
This is before I am born.
She will run into the arms
of my father who is not in this picture.

Her crocheted cap
fell into my hands.
She counted on each loop
of tiny beads. She wore it
to greet my father, it kept
her hair down tight.

The Visit

You come in.
You take the combs out of your hair.
You take off your red beads.
Your skirt is a tent.
Your blouse is a kite.

The children hide in the tent.
You and I run with the kite
we lose it in the high branches.
Be careful.
I am planning to steal your beads.

Gifts

Everything is a gesture
towards your faces,
those great masks with eyes
that burn the heart.
We spend our lives
making you smile:
we do it to make you happy.

We wave colors to make you glad.
Our whole lives we bring nothing
but every scrap
of treasure we can find.

We bring water:
you love the sea.
We bring branches:
you love houses.
We bring rags:
you love costumes.

All over the world
we are planning bank robberies
and christenings
for just one smile.

It's nothing
we do it to make you happy
our whole lives.

The Mother's Poem

One by one the lights go out.
You want to join them,
tuck your head under and sleep.
Already the dreamers
are joining each other in fields,
already they call you,
urging you under their blankets.

You are still awake.
You see your white gown,
a flag in the window.
The dreamers under their trees
eating their night picnics
never pull you in.

The Wife's Poem

The animals are asleep,
the children are covered,
the mother is standing in the hall
leaning her arms into the sky.
She can't sleep. She watches
the dark spaces crack with light.

The husband is moaning.
He is having a nightmare about lions.
Her hand is there, soothing
him over to a dream of water.
She knows this will not last:
she will break or learn to sleep.

Her hand in the future will be settling
small things down in their corners,
folding a narrow blanket,
hemming thin curtains
for the room with one window only
she will live in alone.

Elizabeth Disguised as a Dancer

I see your embroidered legs,
I see the dance you imagined,
I see the sparks on your toes.
You are moving faster than I can
see. I touch the scrap of cloth
you left in my drawer.
I see it crumble: you are
faster away than what you left here.
I see the threads form themselves,
I see them into your cloak,
your disguise on my table.
I see the invisible motion,
I see your dust turn to silk,
fluttering in the cracks of my floor.
I see you scattered in my pockets,
I see you moving again.

Blue Walls

Now you are free to wander in the night
through every corner of the house;
your fingers remember every dark shape.
You lie in your mother's bed and
learn that blue, after all, is only a color,
easy to match, a soothing backdrop
to her insomnia, to her migraine.

Mother was not well. She was in bed.
The blue blanket was folded at her feet.
You had to be very quiet in those times,
you took your shoes off at her door. You played
all by yourself for hours in the linen closet
near the smooth pile of blue towels,
you played being dead covered with talcum powder.

You have grown. It is true you have learned
we live in a human world together;
we have all been lost in our mother's houses
we have all crept down in the night
to put something sweet in our mouths.
You look out from the high windows, now,
and can see other houses, other lights gleaming.

III

The Picnic

We are reaching the landing
where we see spread
the wine and chicken:
this is the French
picnic where you imagined
a boy standing to count stars
he fixed near water.

Behind the scene is another.
Someone is singing
the boy to sleep.
She is his mother.
His head is on her lap,
the cave of his dreams.
Her dress spreads
a cloud on the lawn.

We move back
and see the ring of trees
which keeps the wolves away.

Spring Poem

for John

The city is behind us.
The river is before us.
We walk over the bridge.
Now the edge of the river looks
like the edge of the river at Agincourt:
I tell you the English are winning.

You say these are cliffs.
You are a giant stepping over
chasms, seeking the monster
who sleeps underneath.

This year your first stone
skips five times.
Last year's last stone
skipped twice.

The next bridge takes us back.
The side we cross to now is edged
by yellow stones, stones glowing
with minerals, chemicals, some kind of poison.
We are used to this crossing:
halfway we always stop to count the boats.

Again this year you cry
when we get to the street.
You say you are crying because
a paper cup in the gutter is alone.

In the World

I sit on the floor
near the cage
where a naked woman is keening.
The woman has killed
a little boy.
"He wouldn't stop crying
and I pushed the pillow
on his face to hush him. Now
they say he died
on the way to the hospital.
My boy Chris had to call
the police."

I have nothing to give
but my hand through the bars
which she grips
black-and-blue.

Later, in my own room
at the top of my house
I will sit alone
and very still.

The Marsh

You make yourself new again.
Along your side,
only a thin line marks the scar
where you lay open one whole summer.

Steam rises from your body
in this heat.
You move slowly
you sit up to your chin in yourself.

One morning you are a blue floor.
You are rising, you are learning
to walk again, your feet do not stumble
over the wide roots.

The birds come back,
they tear at you, opening their beaks
in hunger, you feed them.
They will stay.

Again the salt burns in your blood,
but your mud is soft
and you are walking towards the sea.

Nauset Beach

From this nest of sand
she could watch clouds all day.
Or, looking straight,
past the ocean, find land
where salt fields wait
for the women to arrive.

Bending to gather the salt,
the women talk,
their cheeks gleam like diamonds;
making hard light skim over the water
but she cannot hear them.

Tonight she will put back
the salt from her hair,
the sea may carry it there,
all the way over:
the women are always waiting
for every grain to rest.

Swimming at Night

The water carries the body
as it carries other simple beasts:
otter, bear, salmon.

The eyes see only the rainbows
lights from the porches make
on the dark water.

The porches are human —
voices carry over the water,
they are planning to pick berries.

The body in the water smiles as it
turns itself over to float
before it turns to go home.

A Distance from Drowning

A hand can remember
how it feels to be lost
in folds of sand, in the
way water beats
over and over
to your drowning scene.

When dragged under, kick.
Pull up sharp to where the gold
brings ladders to the cave of water;
follow the spear of light.

When you save yourself
they let you tell stories
up and down the beach
all night on the porches
of the fish restaurants.

Summerhouse

This is the outcome of looking
down the dark lawn
towards the black water.
The trees lean, a slow
shadow adrift on the lake
moves with a light of its own.
I am holding the railing
and the touch of dreams
crouches in my fingers:
this is night blindness.

Summer nights I am always alone.
The rising dusk is over.
It is dark now.
I move towards the water
and my walking is slow.

The water is eating the rocks.
No one is here.
If I live through this
I will live forever.

Hibernation

like a secret which spins on alone
lying under oceans of snow
your fingers are weaving lace
your eyes are closed by dreams
you think everything you imagine
will occur in pairs

all around you pairs
of shadows which you alone
are observing I can't imagine
so much solace in dreams
like a cloud of lace
the intricate patterns of snow

moving as still as snow
an old woman wears lace
watching geese fly in pairs
you are charmed by her dreams
and cannot leave her alone
she is replacing all you imagine

later I try and imagine
how it would be if the lace
which covers you was actually snow
which gives nothing in pairs
each flake always alone
fastening you like a hook to dreams

then all your dreams
would be easier to imagine
you would not be alone
every thought would change the lace

every change would break the pairs
and over everything would ride the snow

after all the snow
insinuates into dreams
the irrelevance of pairs
would change everything you could imagine
and the cloak of intricate lace
would remind you of being alone

there are pairs you cannot imagine
even as snow begins to lace
up the dreams which made you alone

Mount Auburn Cemetery

We are in the trees around you.
(This narrow path, the trees close)
You could touch us, now.
You are in Mount Auburn Cemetery.
The city below is in the cup of a spoon
and the trees are huge. They stand in your path.
Auburn is the color of hair you cannot buy.
Henna-rinse is an enamel basin. Hair grows
after you are dead. The scalp burns.
(moss growing on stones as though
  arranged for a crèche in Italy.)
Those who believed, saw us.
Your day will be in the country
pricked by the cold trees;
it will remind you that you must suffer
to be beautiful.
(The cemetery is like a park,
  a wide green space at the edge
  of a city. A place where frogs sleep.)
These foolish animals lie down
only to feed us.

Stones

These stones have not been arranged.
In the country of monuments along every path,
this is the border along the coast,
these are the leavings from the mountain of angels.
The dolphins who copy the angels are sleeping
they do not see me bruise my feet.

When I come here there is no moon.
The stones must be ordered by remembering
light cast by dancers. I cannot find the stone
with only the memory of a streetlamp miles away.
I use my hands to test the weight of each,
I move down closer. I touch them with my tongue.

They taste salt. I believe in mineral properties.
When I find the right monument I will taste it.
I will swallow it, I will carry it in my belly.
I will never drown. The marble will not sink.
I will be buried near water. My hair will grow
when I die, a tree will bloom from my eyes.

The one will be right that holds the light
from the body of a young swimmer who drowned.
The stone will seem at home among the others,
these others that pretend to be children
playing at the water's edge. They are liars.
They are old men who fell out of little boats.

They are old fishermen who never swam:
they hate the sea. The sea is a machine
with long chains to pull them in.
The sea is a machine which rubs them together;

they are polished, gleaming, they are like babies —
if I could see, they would trick me.

Every night I come here and put new stones in my mouth.
Every night the new stones fail me.
In the morning I am never invisible.
I always have to go back along the road,
the fishermen greet me on their way
to the small boats, their eyes are full of light.

Jamaica Plain Poem

We are not dancing
in Leopoldville, on the veranda.
If anything, even there, we would
have had our noses pressed to the windows
looking at the dance floor littered
with broken flowers:
bougainvillea, orchid, gardenia.

Or, leaving the picture palace
we would have walked down the hill
past the Parker House Hotel
where there are no windows,
only a whiff of rolls people eat every day,
not just on Thanksgiving.

We would have gone home on the trolley
to your house in Jamaica Plain,
the house set in, apart from the others,
small and with a real yard.
Your mother and father on the porch
would have greeted us smiling.

Today we break the bread between us.
You tell me stories about Jamaica Plain,
about calling your porch a veranda.
I take the stories into my life.

Love

like wisteria
choking the house, pulling
the porch off,
making the foundation crazy

grey in the off-season
letting you think the birch trees
will make shelter

but the root will not burn out,
the vine comes back
making the house fall down
under the sweetest flower

Nothing
Is Lost

For
John Reynolds Burkhardt &
Rebecca Sweet Burkhardt &
Sarah Hawley Fink

Zhenia

Once when I had bribed the guard
with my last sweater
I was allowed to spend one week
in the long shed
washing dishes.

When the supervisor noticed
that I enjoyed the warmth
from the sink full of water,
I was sent out to serve
the thin cabbage broth
which was the main meal.

A transport of men from the mines
arrived.
Before me stood a bundle of rags
with a gaping hole for a mouth:
"Look, a woman!"
Something possessed me
and I leaned over the table
and kissed him,
full on his bleeding lips.

Barbara's Poem

for Barbara Nielsen Whitcomb on the occasion of her
ordination as Deacon of the Episcopal Church; and for Barbara,
martyr, 6th Century

Your day comes on me
too soon each year
I am not ready.

In your garden
the plants were like jewels, Barbara,
I can still see your hands etched against green;
I miss you.

Why so foolish, Barbara?
You could have stayed safe inside,
sherbets and ice brought in;
you could have spent your life with carpets,
cushions, small boxes of candy, me.

You let the strangers in.
Willful, spoiled, rich man's daughter
indulging yourself with scholars;
at night the lamps burned in the tower.

Jewel of your father's eye:
was it his looks? That simple one
you let come in, finally, alone?
Plain cheese I called him, and you laughed.

Later, I remember you heaving treasures
out the window,

garnishing the corridors with plain wood crosses:
I could have told you where that would end.

A rich girl's fancy: austerity —
and what else I will not mention.
Did you need the third window
so all the world could see through you?
The day you had it built
I said goodbye to you in my mind.

Barbara, I miss you.

I don't think of that day.
Your father, screaming, pulling you by the hair
down to the city
the fire.

The place is empty.
No one is left now,
without you these gardens are haunted.
I am alone.
All day I wander about saying: *Barbara,*
Barbara, where are you!

My rough hands tear the silks you left
crumpled in a corner.
For the sake of a window, foolish one,
for an invisible nothing called soul.

Kathryn Piccard

In the town where I grew up
the trees met overhead, making
a tunnel of green to walk under.
Among us divorce was unheard of;
when my parents did it
I could not see.
That is, I went blind
or partly
or in panic
or faked it. I couldn't see.

There is always one child
who gets teased.

The one thing we did every week
was to go to church Sundays —
I was just a child there
among the other children.
I liked the music and didn't
mind the grown-ups not letting
the children have doughnuts.

And camp, and girl scouts, I loved that.
It was fine. I could
always do that
even when I was blind.

Then I was confirmed. In church,
in Christ's church. Though I took longer
deciding than the others:

it was a matter of finally getting hungry,
needing food that was more than food.

It is not easy to drift into this world.
I had to push my way in,
my white hands clenched.

2

My grandmother flew in a balloon
before I was born.
And I did once, my knee frozen,
the little town below too far:
if you aren't afraid of heights
it is dangerous to be a balloonist.

Now she and I are both priests.
Women priests, two-headed calves,
looking together at twice as many stars.
I am her safeguard on the icy streets,
she is frail, I am as big as she,
she is changing, she is still hurting,
she still wants her sisters to come back.

People don't always choose everything.
I have simply rooted where I was planted.

I am growing here quite well.

I am cracking my share of stones
in this church, in a hundred years

no one will understand
what all this fuss is about.

Maybe we are all stupid together:
all I am doing
is what seems obvious and clear
as bells, ringing to greet us in,
me and grandma,

holding each other's hands
as we slide together
straight into church and
right to the very front with
wine with bread.

Joan of Arc

"For the most part I do the thing which my own nature drives me to do" — Albert Einstein

1

In these green hills
my brother and I run fast.
St. Margaret speaks to me here.
Her face is clean,
I call her light.
She tells me I am chosen
and I know the reason:
strong legs
a sound belly
and straight teeth.

2

I steal my cousin's clothes,
I cut my hair,
I run far.
No one knows me.

3

I must not look back.
But I miss Hauviette most.
In bed at night we played
lovers.
I didn't say goodbye
because I missed her
even before I left.

Before I return she will be fat, she will have children.

4

I had a red dress
I will never wear again.
A rich man gives me

61

a horse, armour, men.

Staying a virgin
turns out to be easy;
I am ugly and healthy.
The silly king himself
hates my peasant breath:
garlic is a useful plant.
In the fields at night
curled up with soldiers,
I reek.

5

After I anoint him
with King David's oil
which is so old and hard
I have to use a gold needle
and prick his forehead,
he goes to sleep.

I eat no meat
take baths, am visited by strange ladies who are
        not interesting.
I have not seen St. Catherine for weeks.

The king plays games in his garden,
and won't fight.

I wear my suit of armour
every day.
My red dress is gone
and I do not want another.

6

Is he a bastard after all?

7

It seems the English at least
take me seriously.
This little round room
is a prison.
But I can see trees.
Sometimes a person can't help
thinking
about her home and her friend.

When I jumped from the tower
I held on, in my mind,
to the corner of my mother's kitchen
where I used to peel vegetables
and so was not hurt.

8

Nothing lasts.
They told me to save France,
so I did.

They didn't tell me
the time would be so short,
so many days spent
sitting in the king's garden.

9

Tomorrow in the flames
I will think of riding my horse,
which was the best of all

and I will
be called brave.

Flower Child

for Linda Kasabian

1
I've put my beads away
and can't remember where
in Death Valley I buried
my box of feathers.

2
You've heard of living
outside the body?
A stranger in the bus station
describes flying over red stones
so you follow that stranger
home like a dog.

3
Anything is possible.
If people do it, it's human.
We were only trying to live forever
like anyone else.

4
If I had been allowed,
that night, to join the others
I would have crossed over
and learned what they know
and won't tell.

But I was on the lawn.

5
So I tell
the story over and over,

my face never stops being pale
I never stop shaking
I hope when I am dead
I will forget
the terrible face of my lover.

Boudicca

"Now she grasped a spear, to strike fear in all who watched her" — Deo Cassius

Hair is a flame,
visible for miles.
A tall woman
carries a shield as tall as she.

This is a cold country.
For many days the blades of grass
are sharp, in the wood houses
winter keeps the people in one place.

Hours of telling
and telling again. Hair,
even hers, singed by the fire
as we lean towards the bright faces.

Hours of telling and telling again,
all the world's known things
carried in our mouths:
the queen in winter takes fire
into her body,
in the field blazes.

Il Marchese

1942
The pilots came and lifted me
beyond the wishes my mother had for my life.

They fell in my field,
I found them in a tangle of string,
wide-eyed:
England.

We buried the evidence.
Two of us carried the third
between us and even his bleeding
lost itself among my grain.
I hid them for three years.
We played bridge.

When it was over my boys went home.

Mother is dead,
the house too big.
I ache when I walk too far.

1950
The Americans have come here
because of the garden,
and for the sake of the health of their children.

The neighbour, Il Marchese
comes for tea.

They find him quaint and marvelous;
kind to the children.

His love of animals
has made him gentle.

He points out nests, snails, ant hills.
He teaches the children:
"Leave a bowl of milk on the steps
and you will see a hedgehog."

    1969
"I've come back to see you, Valdemar,
look, I'm a woman,
here is my little boy:
we've come to see the garden."

On the way to a restaurant
you make the taxi stop in the park
at the center of the city.

You open a large wicker basket
full of rats:
"They like the city best" you say.

Out of love
I do not scream.

Domina

for Sylvia Plath

A woman walks in a small section
of the world.
She carries something sharp:
her hands are bleeding
and the sun beats through
slivers of glass, setting fires.

For the broken glass
you carry, I forgive you.
Though in trying to get rid of it
you have pushed in deep
into the hearts of people
who would have shown you light
without hurting your eyes.

We who would love you burn;
you are made not to see us
and in our generation
we have lost the trick
of knowing how to feed
those who never die.

You are among us so close;
and here we are, arms full of roses
we're ready to give you,
and milk, and a blue bowl —
if you would only look.

Put yourself among clouds, then;
there is your bed
there is your blanket

you can look at us in safety
we cradle, we rock you to sleep.

A woman walks between two sections
of a small city
in such confusion:
takes light into her own hands
and is forgiven, even by strangers.

Letter from the Colonies

I have not known such cold, sister,
we are locked in each other's arms
for weeks here, the ground is iron.

There is a certain loveliness:
you should see the sun on ice,
though our eyes ache looking.

We will stay. There have been not a few
deaths and the ground is too hard for graves;
but we will stay. There is some food.

The savages have tamed the ground
enough for that, we profit and learn;
we are as angels beside them.

I am certain you should come —
a few winters away we will have made
dominion of every thing we see.

Angels

God's messengers on earth
are terrible and those who look
at their faces become blind and go crazy.

They are light-as-razor, light
as that-which-burns, they are not visible.

A coal burning in the mouth
is like an angel, and at night
they steal the children who die.

People have walked, bandaged
for miles in the desert
after speaking with only one angel.

Good angels are more like fire;
harder than bad angels
and more dangerous.

Bad angels are only angels
who live in dark places
blind and trapped.

No one has seen an angel for years.
They are away, dancing and not dancing.

Neighbour

I worry about her.
She seems so nervous about the children,
never letting them out of her sight.
She has a new baby but has grown so thin
she's lost all her milk.

In the blizzard, the only time
we ever spoke, I frightened her.
She wouldn't take milk from me,
even for the baby, who was crying.
The husband walked for miles in the storm
to get the milk. He wouldn't speak at all.

I believe she's crazy, as much as she
believes I am. I wonder if she watches
when I take my clothes off at night.

Or maybe the husband watches the woman next door
getting undressed and his wife knows,
which makes her unable to eat solid food, which drives
        her crazy.

Prison Visit

for Ella Ellison

Some people know how to wait.
You wait,
you wait on a green bench near the trees.
You are waiting for the trees to move,
to lead you out
past the fence.

When I visit you
we lie on our backs and see
a tangle of branches against the sky.
I say they are a wonderful basket for catching fish.

You say they have caught you
and that looking at branches
without the fence behind them
stings your eyes,

that the fence at least
makes you not forget
where you are.

Three Ravens

I have black hair
and I saw three ravens
and I know what that means:
I'm getting out soon.

My last furlough
I got married
(only of course, not legal
it was with a woman)
Anyway, she's going to look out for me, she says.

My husband used to raise his finger to me
like I was a kid.

It was because I tried to hide the body,
they gave me such a stretch. If I had
only stabbed him and cried it wouldn't
have been so bad, my lawyer said. But
my kids are grown, they don't miss me.

My son didn't think I'm a witch
but I told him about a certain hailstorm
which he called me long distance
to say was true.

They're all scared of me,
all the people
a good woman and I say those three birds
prove it.

The Weaver

She doesn't move much.
The skeins are set in baskets,
spilling colors into her lap.
They glow. She chooses by setting
them side by side in the sun.

She has sky-blue,
blood-red, snail shell color,
color for under a stone,
the shade for a child's throat,
dark green of the footprint on grass.

The patterns are subtle, they change
very little. Mistakes lie in a heap,
banners fly from the window; child, root, fish, all
woven together, the dead and the living.

The Woman Who Knits

Her tension is even,
she is the French farm wife
(mother of an idiot savant)
who leans each day
against her white-walled house
and knits a sock
turning the heel
as the mailman turns the corner.

At night her boy sleeps
on the floor near the oven,
her husband's heart hammers
against her back.
She keeps awake,
imagines the new pattern: cast on, divide evenly —
knit two, pearl two
until sock reaches desired length,
use double-pointed steel needles.

The Spell

for *Patricia Cumming*

I want to know how you could
and stay in the world:

a woman who goes to the store
to buy apples for her daughters

comes home and puts them in a wooden bowl,
her daughters eat them,

goes up to her room
and makes spells against pain.

Trying this has made more than
one woman turn to stone,

another, for example, spends years
making her tongue say all eyes are not tricks.

Lot's Wife

A quiet garden:
lemon trees in pots
big as children
learning to walk
but with hands still shaped
like starfish.

A girl is climbing,
wet bark between her knees;
frogs small as flowers
swim in the pond.

If you look back
you will turn into salt.

The Bad Mother

Remember that in the evening, just at supper
we would sometimes see
children burning.

You were just a baby.
I would rock you in front of the TV
your father would come home late
from his work, and sometimes
not for days.

I would rock you there and
each time they showed the dead people
or a young boy screaming
I would stiffen and you would start to cry.

Then later, when we were alone, all the time,
the walls would collapse
around me and I would have gone myself
straight into the picture and stood
with the others.
You crying in the evening had become
a pattern of living.

I was the good mother.

The bad mother left her children behind
and was on television
becoming a fanatic,
crazy: she spent two years
in prison, not eating,
while her children were home, alone, waiting
for their mother, the bad mother.

They kept
a Christmas tree standing for two years
until she came back.

Siren

The wreath of flowers around her head
is wilting
but her eyes still burn.
She stands on a small island
and the waters are rising.
He wants to take a little boat
there and lift her in it,
row safely back to the wooden pier
where they sell taffy.
If he can get something sweet
into her mouth she may speak,
she may wrap him into her cloak,
she may be still.
But his hands are bleeding,
it's cold,
she throws rocks.

Clairvoyance

She is afraid
or a tower of strength
turning, before his eyes, to salt.

She wishes the crystal
hanging in the window
could transmit more than light.

Wise lovers know the future:
journeys, separation.

Aubade

Even in China
it cracks us apart.
Dust is already pouring
over the children's faces
and we can see it.

The room fills with light
as we move away.
Now we are two unknown people,
putting on socks and shoes.

Water

You wrench away from me fast
then come back to my door
with bowls of water, not milk;
not even a flower
floats on the surface.

I want no water.
In the desert the water is buried
inside eggshells. Only the people
who live there know where it's hidden
and they don't tell strangers.

Or I want all water,
an ocean floor, maybe, where no one
hides anything, where survival
means being able to grow fins.

But I'm here. It's raining.
Every cupped thing in the garden is spilling over.

Amnesia

First, the name of your father,
then your house.

You are standing among trees,
they glow, they are covered
with a veil of ice.
The ground beneath your feet
is white, you are in snow.
You wear a white dress,
you wear dancing shoes.

But you are among the trees,
the heel of your dancing
shoe is broken,
you carry it in your hand.

There is blood on the hem
of your white dress.
The dress is a costume.

There are two pairs of footprints
behind you, leading back
through the trees to a white
spread of lawn.

The snow is making you blind.

One pair of footprints does not lead
as far as you have come.
Part of the way the heel
of your shoe was not broken.

Walking towards the house
you forget you were running,

you forget the color of your hair.

Closer, you forget if you are big
or small. You forget the heel
of your shoe is in your hand.

Near the door
people are gathered,
they watch you stumble toward them.

They are holding blankets,
they are holding their
arms out wide to gather
you in. They are strangers.

A man wraps you in blankets,
a woman smooths out your hair.
She wants to take you upstairs
to the bed and give you hot milk,

she wants to know where
is your lover.

Hide Out

You decide to hide near a river.
You build a house of reeds,
one room, an upside-down basket.

No one can find you
any more. Your shoes are worn out.

There are fish to eat from the river,
the water is clear,
you can walk alone for miles, seeing
nothing but the faint marks
of your own footsteps.

You can hide out forever;
this is a place no one knows.

Though at night, hugging your own body
you can hear the otters in the distance:
barking, coming closer.

Loss

Your diamonds are lost,
you aren't here any more:
we sold your last skirt;
seller and buyer blind to the cloth:

you aren't here any more
even the children have covered their ears
seller and buyer blind to the cloth
the gold thread is not visible

even the children have covered their ears
glass houses surround us, diamonds are for music
the gold thread is not visible
some of us think we remember the way

glass houses surround us, diamonds are for music
fish do not speak, wishes are not granted
some of us try and remember the way
water beat when you drowned, the flat sound.

Remedies

for Dashiell Hammett

A long sea-voyage:
lean on the polished railing
in your white shawl:
spit into water.

A revolution:
learn to hide in the jungle
where people can be mistaken
for a new kind of flower

A new lover:
lie in a hammock
smoke opium together
dye your hair orange, curl it.

A shopping expedition:
in the most elegant store,
buy a red dress, a fan —
a pearl handled revolver.

Lament

You are farther away
than an island of black grapes
and the boat
which makes an icy crossing
as it approaches:
the church, the house, the vineyard: —
so far.

In the Mines

1 Another Place

Give over to the strange chairs,
the soft bed. Something
different for breakfast
or no breakfast or at a different time.

The confusing location of the new bed
windows on the wrong wall
the wrong tree.

Awake, stiff, uncertain
about where to put the dirty sheets —
to wash a cup or leave it.

Far from home, among strangers
light changes everything.

2 Leaves

Fill your mouth with berries,
stain your hands and lips
purple, come to the pond —
walk in, not looking
at where you put your feet.

You are learning
that a tangle of roots
connects the entire
round world.

3 *Green Mountains*

Green mountains have closed eyes.
When they awaken we will know giants again,
they will walk about
splitting open the ground.

We will live in caves again
in rooms carved by water
we will taste those fish,
the blind ones that glow.

The mountains wait only for the buzz of voices to
change.

A deeper sound will wake them,
will open the dark world.

4 *Outside*

You are in a world of strangers
made of glass
and they can break you.

Your face is a mask too,
you aren't the only one who sees
flames in other people's eyes.

When you buy a dress covered with roses
realize that someone with the same confusion

has gone before you, pasting them on.

Remember the lights at night
show the rooms of houses
where people live, lifting spoons
to their mouths, as you do sometimes, feeling
the warmth on their tongues.

Remember these things,
learn them: step out
and look into mirrors, into windows:
fragility is enduring.

5   *Autumn Sky*

Look at it.
You may be saved.
The wind comes from water.
Away from this sharp grass
a house near the ocean waits.

It is your house
if you make it.

The same sky which covers you now covers this
house.

You can go there,
even walking
one step at a time.

Before winter you can be making soup

on a clean stove with sweet
smelling walls around you.

6   In the Mines

Make no mistake, this tunneling will be a success
you will find an end.
As by putting one foot
in front of the other, following the edge of sand
you could step
in every country.

When you emerge,
fists full of hard rock,
you will own light.

In the mines it is always dark.
The treasure is not visible
but it surrounds you.
Take it.

Remember only that it's like
digging a hole to China
on a dry, hot day
and reaching, after a long time, water.

Red Boots

We lived in palaces of stone
before we were born.
Leaning our arms
on the window-sills
we could see our mothers,
running, wearing red boots

True Lies

Always a stranger among us:
hidden pockets in your coat —
you are ready to move
at a moment's notice.

That's the story you tell us,
flaming your hair with your long fingers.
But it's a lie.

You have no secrets in your coat,
no small tickets folded away.
Even when you cut your hair,
you stayed.

If you burn down the house
and the blackberry bushes
and let the pine trees come
you won't get away.

There are no special papers:
you are here with us, you will stay with us.
The stories you tell are only meant to scare us;
they are not necessary
we cannot abandon you.

Where

oak tree,
elm tree,
under the porch
out by the trash barrels
in the upstairs closet
where the blankets are

leaving small marks
until they become strange,
tall, owners of faces.

Faces

Dead people play
quiet games: push-the-plants-up
and hide-the-body

so no one wants to plant
bulbs deep there.

Soon their faces melt
they are hard
to remember, like the moon,
round the invisible.

Sarah's Place

Tom boy
small girl
Queen Victoria
dead, six days old:
the other children
play ball here, your grave, third base.

Rebecca

"All the tired horses in the sun" — *Bob Dylan*

At the actual moment
of your birth, your head coming
out from between my legs,
I sang.

All through the morning of the first day
I watched.
Perfect daughter,
rose, rose, rose.

All through the morning of the first day
I watched
and saw, as afternoon came,
a shadow pass over your face.

You seemed so fierce.
Evening, night, morning,
your anger made you strong.

The evening of the second day
your face turned away.

You pushed off on some journey,
leaving behind even the moon
which came up orange that night
pulling you to another place
and a terrible new smile.

Grief

A grey stalk in water
sends out a flower:

nothing is lost forever.
The ones who sleep underground

come back in dreams,
wearing the faces of strangers.

We have to learn again and again
what to keep, what to throw away.

The Third Book

(Uncollected Poems)

The Muse

Muse

She does not enter my body
and she does not tell my feet how to dance.

I know that she is a woman,
I had expected a handsome stranger.

Our relationship is not harmonious,
that is, she resents,

I think, herself not having
a handsome stranger to boss around.

So she comes with her hot knives
or she fastens her teeth on my wrist

or she stands with her face
pressed against my window

trying to shatter glass
by turns with ice, with fire.

Childhood, Family

Apricot Tree

I could lie on my bed
and watch on the white wall

the movement of shadow leaves
from the garden just behind the curtain.

I could not believe the source
was a tree that in the morning

and outside had green and sharp
pointed leaves — it was an apricot

tree and when the days were hot
the fruit would ripen and two golden

apricots would be set before me.
I never learned the connection:

leaf, tree, shadow, fruit.

The Garden

Do you remember the garden? If not mine,
any garden. The way light is different each day?

Terrible things can suddenly happen.
In one night slugs have eaten the bright leaves.

Is lace also a version of what
                          eats the heart?
A kind of leaf eaten away for lack of salt,
for lack of witness?

On the garden steps my mother gives Lydia
a bottle of Lilly vitamins.
                       Little orange footballs.
I take them too:
that time Marcello and I took them together
just before supper and were given one bite
of fruit before the meal, to kill the taste.

                       Do you remember Marcello?
Only a small boy in a large house. What did he
look like?

The garden was in Italy.
It had a crooked swing.
Children who have children now played there.
They have left behind the ghosts
                       of their child-selves.

The small girl learns
to make lace, which will be put in a box.
Even before she marries she will lose it.

The small boy takes vitamins.
Before he grows he will have lost his mother,
Lydia.

Gold

Mother brings white pills
wrapped in a lace handkerchief
on visiting day.
She buys them on the black market.

All afternoon, we sit in the sun
in warm and cold weather
on wooden chairs, wrapped in blankets.
The nuns come out with bowls of fruit
for all the children.

So many children!
Always a new one
to take the place of the one just gone.

The nuns tell lies:
"Maria has gone to live with the angels."

So it doesn't seem so bad,
smuggling those pills
to my little sisters.

When the gold is gone
we will be well;
gold is for saving children from death:

when we are saved
there'll be no more need for it.

The Spoiled Child

I'd be a liar if I said
I didn't love that life.
Alone, kept safe
from the rough games.

Lydia would bring strawberries
or sweet ladyfingers
to reward me for not being
Hans, the bad German boy.

No one since has given me such
good things and I miss
the green leaves of the almond tree,
Lydia and her soft hands.

The Swing

the swing was not hung straight
to begin with
        I held her very tightly
on my lap   I did not ever mean
to let her go

        blood
        on the soft lip
of the youngest child
her hand-smocked dress   (from England)
        stained and torn
her screams make all the family come running
out to see   what have I done
        to her this time

she will overtake me
           one day she stares
beyond me on the airport runway
her blue cape lifts in the wind
        all eyes turn toward her
who is this beauty
        this elegant stranger?

Ravioli Fiorentini

The shape of land changes.
Great yellow machines
have flattened the olive grove
I thought Jesus lived in
(with that purple light
coming over the hillside
when the sun set
how could it not be true?)

We spread the white linen
under the olive trees
and ate Lydia's green ravioli cold.

She has not said a word
for thirty years. I make
green ravioli, my hands
repeat the gestures exactly,
make the dimples
with the wet tines of a fork.

A hill blooms on my tongue
I know the secret ingredient
that flavors this meal
faithfully, faithfully executed.

ᕗ III

Houses

Arrival

after Apollinaire

The beautiful
unknown person
will not meet you
on an island.

Nor, despite the yearning
you have cultivated
all your life

will the little blonde child
hand you a bouquet
of wild flowers.

Rather, you will arrive
slightly fatigued
from your journey,

find the pump rusty —
you must oil it and pump
water into the bucket
with your own hands.

The New House

They had been traveling for days
following the river
climbing the foothills
the wet green leaves
closed over their heads   the ground
brown and wet
                she was getting tired
she was finding it hard to remember
              why they had come
ripe berries had become dull
to her tongue   the small fishes grilled
over the coals at night
                 only made her hungry
for bread.

             He was not tired
his hands tied back branches
             he could imagine the higher peaks
and the pass they would find later
and the valley below
               full of fruit
               of calm animals
and where they would sleep together
the wonderful bed of fur and branches.

And they did go on
              until it was so
though at dusk even far in the future
              she never told
about having wished to remain
still in one place
             and for a long time
in the old garden, to have heard
the human voices not so distant.

The House

there is a house
where people sit in darkness

light is swallowed
in every room

the embroidered slippers
tell nothing about feet,

about hands that put them on
about steps in that dance

and these sleepers do not dream
on the banks of the river,

their bread is stone
their meat is dust.

Three Houses

The three houses in my dream
are not only in a town
or in a field, but near the ocean.

The interiors are ideal:
wide floorboards, muslin curtains,
cats sleeping near the fireplaces.

I buy them all, and though the bed's
too narrow, I dive down and hear
the musical clocks, the cat's purr.

South Window Upstairs

Before summer is half over
the trees change.
One dies
while near it the apple tree
fattens its fruit
and the oak leaves on the third tree
are grey with heat.

Through the opening
these trees give
the small house no one lives in
seems closer,
in a town full of derelicts
the only one
who still expects occupation.

Pastoral

The tomatoes are splitting
open on the vine.

Branches force open the windows
of the house with no one inside.
The walls crack, birds live
in the eaves. The simple work
of making things clean is not known here.

The house full of flowers
and bread is far, in another country.

Island

Mid-August the sun is flat
hardening each shadow

we are still looking for water
haven't yet begun fastening the roof

carry rocks in our hands
are these enough?

This must be a game to us,
not survival, not wind

power or strong shelter
to save us from the future.

We pretend life is simple
on an island, but summer

is dark here too and the men
get drunk and fall on the pier

and the women stay inside
fry fish, boil potatoes.

Bones

The hand that learns
one small gesture over and over

the cave insulated with moss;
the condominium

        ozone, radium, a life spent
        repeating: " light bends. "

The clean room
        (pride of the woman who cleans it,
        who buys a dozen oranges on her way
        to work and puts them in her green
        plastic net bag, strong, well made;
        who makes the room gleam)

the room where there are always
enough paper clips
always a sharp pencil.

The junction between the hand
holding the pencil
and the mind which governs how the pencil moves
sharp
tight as a rubber band:
mathematics, lace, music.

Nothing dies here.
      Light as pin
      point moves with precision
      clearer than Bach which requires
      hands to play the music,

hands not perfect as this movement
can be.

We can build a house in the green hills,
in the green hills, it can glow,
the parts gleaming, systems pulsating
the beat of its own heart
will go on beyond the frailty of our bodies,
our bodies which stumble and sometimes fail us

surround the perfect bones we can leave behind
in one moment: the white grid;
a cage for the world.

~§ IV
Griefs

Advice

I am not going to give you any advice
because in a moment you can lose all the beautiful things
you have loved.
And then it will be hard
and for a long time
to look at the sky
and the clouds will be your enemy
and the moon will be a knife.

The Lost World

close
        below the surface
    of the meadow
                    with its red smear
of poppies   or the lake
                            skaters
make dull with their blades
    you think you see it
                    like the fixed
smiles on the faces
        of the couple
married   four thousand years
                    when you left the room
where they live
                    how could you know
they would follow you?
                    even here
on the other side of the world
                            even as you mark
what you have seen
                    knowing when you return
with witnesses
                    there is only a field
the frozen lake.

The Value of Literature

On certain nights
I remember this:

flat on the ground
my mouth open
swallowing stones
rather than speak

poisoning the earth
with my grief.

On Losing the Miracle in China

After we saw
the old woman
build a dam
alone, moving the earth
in buckets slung
over her bony shoulders

we could imagine
even stars, their courses
changed, the bitter stars
that guide us, suddenly lifting
our feet up
to where clear water
grows sweet melons
and at last even
the language of birds
revealed to us, clear and certain.

O! how ardently
we strained to hear
that music which would teach our hands
to weave the silken net!

Around my neck on a velvet ribbon
a silver circle, folded in on itself,
that Irene brought back
from actual distant China,

unfolded: to become scissors
to use when embroidering
thousand-league slippers for women
to stride in, singing.

The day I lost them
I learned I cannot manage

124

even the most simple of tricks,
keeping hold of an amulet

against the tangle of losses,
the lies holding up a wooden bridge
which breaks
when I want to cross it.

To a Friend

Dear lock-the-cellar-door
against the wind
dear member of the kindness tribe,

who puts the peonies
together with their greenery
near the window

so strangers too
can see a beautiful sight in the world.
What can I tell you?

That your tribe is dying out?
That you alone
don't know it?

We tasted ripe pears
once, sitting on a low stone wall
near the garden.

Now it is time to forget
even the shapes our names make
in the air.

The barbed thorns of the blackberry
no longer give us fruit
and will not flower next spring.

The Shy Woman

As I get older I get worse,
not better.

       Now when the man
at the party puts his hand
on my waist or presses his tongue
into my mouth

        my blood freezes
and I have no sound to make.

Bad

Remember when you dreamed
day after day
about being really bad?
Bad like the girl
who got pregnant at age sixteen
or the guy who set fires
or that terrible boy, Christopher,
who killed his parents.

When you listened for the next
Buddy Holly song on the radio
far into the night
and dreamed about running
away to Greenwich Village?

But you never did.
Listening to Buddy Holly at 2 AM
on a schoolnight
was as bad as you could manage
and you never even got caught.

So you swallow your life
like a whole apple
you can't taste.

Other people do things
you watch them.

And you become a most wonderful liar.

Domestic Violence

With no pen or paper
how can I write the terrible poem
of domestic violence?

How at night, walking
I see through the half-parted curtains

the children awakening
to the bad dreams
and the mothers and fathers

fighting again and again
the father's fist
the mother's wish

the knives waiting
in the kitchen.
Someone throws a rock

through my window
so I hide in the dirty clothes
with no pen, no paper.

Manchester, 1856

At night
from the high windows
I look down
into the city and see
the flames
so beautiful!

Beyond the dreams
of all the sleeping kings
these buildings
where so many people work —

how must it feel
to be one of them?

knowing the strength
of his hands changes
the world?

An Evening

On his way home the impulse
to keep driving past the house,
past the place where the trees
thin out to hard sand,
where the car can't go anymore:

he'd rest his forehead
on the steering wheel
wondering, where is the life?
Where is the life someone is weaving
for me? Where is the bowl
of canned peaches, and the spoon
clinking against the white china
while behind me someone is singing
under her breath?

Back at the house, she waits.
The hot pillow of boredom
presses against her face,
the bad spring hurts her ribs.

She tries to remember, what did I do
before with all this time?
The bathroom mirror does not help;
these aren't the eyes
of the girl who hung,
upside down, her knees
hooked round the branches
of the apple tree in fullest bloom,
singing, singing, I bought my love
a packet of pins...

Fire

1
No one was home
the teenagers next door
were flipping out
cigarettes on to the roof.

So the building caught fire
it was mid-afternoon,
the firemen put it out
right away.

Later, I helped the woman
carry down her charred furniture.

You can never get rid of the smell.

2
I was ten
when the field
next to our house
caught fire.

I was home alone,
the smell of the fire
was stronger
than Vicks VapoRub.

I watched at the window,
rubbing my oily chest
until the firemen went away.

No one knew
I was there.

3

Once a crazy girl
burned her wrist
with a candle.

She wrapped her arm
in a wet towel
and came to my door.

She showed me her wrist—
charred black.
That smell was worse.

Granite

The trees, which darken the night
turn green and separate
in one moment.

Silence is banished
to the future
I'm trying to wait for

dull with too much
I've seen and heard
this whole night.

And for that have only
the wish not to lie
on this slab of granite

filled with cracks
in which more occurs
than I can gather.

I want the smooth hot rock
I can lie all day on
and feel my body.

Moon

there had been no night
like that night

no moon
since that moon shone

that moon burned
making the river red
tearing the mother's arms
as though the child was
water   as though the beating heart
was the tide

Salamander

Sweetest salamander,
empress of fire, when you
own all, take the dust that is so fine,
like bolts of silk,
weave what palace or labyrinth
pleases you; all the rest
of us shall be the same one.

No tongue, no hand, no foot
to stop your work, to slow
the heap of empty minarets.

Hawkins Point

The grey house, clapboard with blue
shutters, is ours. Last on Bay
Road with the orchard behind
and sloping down beyond it is the field, then
water opens out, the small boats
we fish in, with names like
"Liberty" and "Arabella" and "Star."

We have made the good life here.
This is our secret.

My father goes to work in summer
when light first cracks, changing the black
orchard to green. In winter I hear him
put his shod feet down and stomp
to the kitchen. Then all our breath
smokes out except there. At the stove
Mother has already fried a batch of golden
crullers or apple fritters, and Henry,
my brother, sits at the round table
his plate already cleared for more.

We have made the good life here.
Go in the yard. Stand near the garden
fence and look over.
Here is the vegetable patch
you have dreamed of all your life.
The rich black dirt we feed fish heads to:
the beefsteak tomatoes like rubies,
almost breaking red to some other
dark sweet color — the greens running
from the clear delicate curls
on the sweet pea vines to the dark
spinach and collard colors.
Squash, pumpkin, musk

137

melons and the patch of sweet round
watermelons; cucumbers. Beets, beans,
snap and bush. Over in the corner
herbs grow in and between and all around
the annuals — zinnias with faces
big as pie plates, asters, bachelor
buttons. The strange morning-glories
climb round the whole fence looking
as though they'll blow away
at the next puff of breeze but stronger
than the wire that holds them up.

And the whole back half is planted
with Country Gentleman corn
(and did you hide, a small child,
in the corn patch, down, close
to the ground where the ants
are building to scale the Valley
of the Kings and as you watched
you forgot to listen for your name
until you came in late for supper
on that summer night so your Mother
gave you just a bowl of milk
and bread to eat but later snuck you
a wedge of blackberry pie? Do you
remember the tall green pillars
in the patch of Country Gentleman?)
This is our secret...

This is the house Great-grandfather built.
After Slavery. Near water, near
where fish jumped into his straw hat,
where you wade in the clear waters of the Chesapeake

and crabs follow you home to jump in the pot.
This is the good life. Aunt Florence has a cow.
No one else wants to live here, at the wrong end
of Baltimore, beyond the bus, where it's
casual plumbing and berries
are gone wild and where no house
has a marble stoop. Boys in overalls
carry fishhooks and jacknives. We girls
wear cotton dresses, faded with washing and sun.
But we are clean. Even our feet. We know
the secret life of the snail. We know
how to prune the peach tree so each fruit
has full sun and we know how to trap
the golden fruit in jars for the cellar
so we eat midsummer even at Christmas dinner.

Can we blame our fathers for keeping it secret?
Our mothers for rejoicing when work came
closer to keep us from having to travel?

Charles W. Jones stands in the orchard.
I, Rachel Hannah Wilkins walk toward him.
Mother, Lucie Marie, born Hawkins, holds the lace
handkerchief her grandmother made on the wagon
she came here on. Do I remember that there were fewer
blossoms on the trees that year? Or do I make
that up to tell my daughter so she will think
I was a noticing person, even when content?

In any case, that wedding is the last
time I remember clearly the swell and hum
bees and blossoms make. And thinking
"That is a marriage too," and hoping
no bee would fall down the back of my white

lawn dress and sting me as Aunt Florence
had been stung once in church by a wasp...

The truth is I only remember the bees,
swollen blossoms and the daze my mind was in,
like any other bride (later, I always wanted
another wedding, so I could remember it better).

I know that nothing is as good as I remember
that life was. There must have been worry.
(Henry moving away. My Mother getting sick.
Charles W. and I having a bad time,
until we learned. The first baby, a boy,
born dead. Scratching at the wallpaper
in my grief until it tore right off
and Charles W. cried too.)
No. Even death in that time seems
only a stranger, who wraps for a moment
your heart in his barbed wire. Our secret
part of town held too many pleasures.
We ladies wearing hats with our cotton dresses
and who ever noticed the white gloves
getting so we had to wash them every day?

To us it seemed a blessing. Factories
protecting us all around. Charles works in one,
all the men have jobs. All the women garden.
And we know we're safer than before. Our
part of town is less easy to find. Strangers
do not come on picnics here, or go fishing,
or even pick the berries. Here is a meadow.
Here is clean water. Here we grow smug.
God is paying us back with fruit and fish and land
and the shadow of the angel's wing hovers over our roofs.
It is God's great cleverness to let most people

think it's only the smokestacks.
We know the angel is shielding us,
when our eyes sting, we know the tears of joy
are in us. And in living memory the fireflies
were gone one year, but they came back. If
the peepers make less noise this year, that is a blessing
too. It's easier to sleep now the nights are quiet.
We have made the good life here.

Can we blame our husbands for keeping their jobs?
Our selves for rejoicing that our children sit
on the back steps of our own houses,
eating slabs of warm bread with blackberry jam?

It did take us a while.
Not from ignorance or being stupid
(nor far from the world, really).
Love and greed, kept us, like most people, going.

My father nods off in front of the TV news,
losing his hair, losing time, losing memory...
I don't bother much with the garden.
My daughter, Catherine Ann brings home
a handful of berries. But they're dusty, bitter,
not worth the bother. Does any of us
even notice the day we eat the last
of the home-canned tomatoes?

Charles W., foreman, drives us to the Safeway
in the Oldsmobile with push-button windows
and I can buy in one afternoon canned goods
that would have taken me weeks to put up.
One day, Henry is coming to visit and we buy
chicken and peaches and a good bottle of Bourbon
whiskey the boys can sip on the back steps

after the picnic. It's the last day
I can remember knowing we lived in a good place.

Charles W. and Henry are hosing down the car.
I'm frying up the chicken.
Catherine Ann is churning the peach ice-cream.
Father is watching the TV news
which is how we hear Hawkins Point is the chosen place
for Maryland's new model chemical dump. Already
the site of so much poison. And the few residents
will be justly compensated and removed from this
         great danger.

The maroon paint on the Oldsmobile
comes off, as I watch from the window,
in blisters. The men just turn the water off
and come inside.

The Book of Maps

So if ice is on the road?
So if trees are only summer's shadow?
So if this wind steals bread
from the mouths of the hungry?

The lamb and the lion
lie down in different weathers,
the lamb suffers to stand
while sleet stings her face.

The lion is golden,
her hot breath, her hot breath
blooms in another country.

The saints were lion hearted
and sweet as lambs
and roses, those thornless beauties...

The maps name places
not the hungry. The dead
saints are bloodless,

they died before
the book of maps was made. We murder
nameless corpses,

cruelty so dull
without the saving grace
of the known body.

Drought

And the day, like all other days,
brings sunrise,
gold honey pouring over our faces

and we find it not beautiful
not the radiant source of king or life.
The queen weeps. But no tears

flow down the dusty cheeks,
and in her grief if she tears her flesh
no drops of blood to soothe her breast.

Nothing. With no water the shimmer of gold
stops every throat from singing.
Our bones are turning, from this day, to stone.

Black Bread

He would not eat,
the loaf round and firm,
fresh as the sweet
butter near it — taste as sharp
as the knife beside it.

Death eats no bread
only the body
after the red jet of blood
has fallen still on the white neck
beneath. Or the woman
with beautiful hair who turns
finally, her face to the wall.

~§ V

Love and Silence

Spelling Our Language

1

Yours is ice on the tongue
we learn it young
and spend our lives unwinding
skeins of it to knit our own
spells.

2

During a rainstorm
on a Sunday
afternoon under the tent
of a white sheet
your fingers on my skin:
afterwards I tell you
go away
I will not learn to talk.

Frontier

The edge of the garden
where the weeds are menacing
the lawn, the tendrils are reaching
out to twist around the rose arbour
with its blowsy old roses. The afternoon
with its fat bees, the hum
and the thick pollen hanging
on air. Blinded by this haze
you prick your finger to the bone,
stumble into the wild patch.

Wild Grapes

He walks away from the house,
leaving the children behind
because their hands are sticky.

His hands touch paper
after supper his napkin is clean
the wind blows leaves away from his hair.

Coming home
he fills his arms with wild grapes
to show he lives among people.

When she walks to the field
she does not see the tangle
of wild grapes beside the path.

She does not stop until, finally,
a tree is there.

This tree lifts up
the land around it, moves
in the dark. Leaning against it
and looking up she sees
the branches make a snare;
she could get caught there
and stay, always.

On the way back
she scratches her hands bloody
picking wild grapes, eating,
staining her mouth, her hands
stain the door.

Careless Love

I look at the roses
and birds on the wallpaper.
I remember the room my grandmother
called "the breakfast nook."

My mind
often wanders like this.
I tend to forget what I am doing, I submit
quietly to the intensity above me.

I avoid getting a cramp
in my leg.

I hear the man moan. Finally
my husband has reached his climax
and now for a moment
he is a total stranger.

It is in this moment that I hold
his shoulders tightly against my breasts
in this moment I would like to forget
about the roses, the birds, the cramp in my leg.

But I don't take care.
By the time I notice
the present moment, it's over.

I am the girl in the breakfast nook window
not listening to what is said.

Polecat

If, on any night, you had awakened
with that same breathing,
reached over with your arm
to cover my body, lost,
as when you did awaken thus one time...

For a moment
the breathing filled
the darkness of this room
the cave of eider-down
we burrow in trembled with that breathing;
the chickens were disturbed.

So we ran outside. Before I let the lantern
drop you shot the polecat, clean
between the eyes, a perfect hit.

Arms round each other, on that moonless night
we went to bed again. Your body loosened,
your quiet breathing like an open hand,
resting in a picnic meadow.

I know my eyes are not a yellow fire. I heard
you once excited, breathing. Love, I thought,
love come to rise me up, love creatures bear
in bodies, for each other. But they are lost,
as we will never be, in light or darkness.

And I did let the lantern drop
but only after the bright shot had rung
and met the mark.

The Truth of These Warlike Women

in April the kings
of the bordering lands
assemble   after the queens
have chosen the other maidens
                  cast lots for their valentines

                  this one month they feast
                  they drink their wines
in abundance

                  then the moon being down
they all depart
to their own province.

if they conceive and be delivered
of a son
          they return him to the father
but if of a daughter
          they send a gift
          unto the begetter

          that they cut off the dug
of the breast I do not find
to be true

                  if in the wars
they take any prisoners
                          they accompany with those
but in the end   for certain
                  they put them to death.

Homecoming

I come back
looking for your mouth
and the taste of your sweet tongue
like sugar to me.

Outside the neighbours
are singing to call
their children in, while we
inside the house cannot speak.

How many times at dawn
have I awakened to feel the weight
of your outstretched arm
on my belly?

I saw a peacock on a lawn once
and my throat closed.
I cannot say anything
by way of greeting.

Agriculture

Must have come from birds
the way they scatter seeds
about the world, planting
whole forests on the fly

and sit so patiently waiting
for the egg to ripen

Recovery

She places the green fields
in her apron pocket,
in thousand-league-sandals
walks through the broken world,
puts dry sticks in sand
and the forest begins to bloom.

Silence

I want to live in this forest forever —
become a saboteur. Derail the train,
remain behind to detonate the charge
that blows the bridge sky high.

Corpses of small animals
litter the path before me.
I turn back to the hostel;
dark bread and cheese, smoked bits
of fish and meat. The boy I love
in silence.

Down a bank of sweet fresh grass
we roll together, clasped tightly
in each other's arms forever
locked without a word.

I want my body to do the talking,
I like a lover
who doesn't speak my language.

I will build a wall
with my own hands. My lover
will die in another country,
at the stadium. His mouth will bloom.

I never learn to speak
when I make love. I smoke
the post-coital cigarette in silence.
This body is my only instrument, I learn
no other language.

Joys

Bread

Risen bread
is love's silk mountain
it is the bread itself

which loves the baker
the sleeves of her shirt
her wide blunt hands

these lovers meet
near the oven's red eye
they do not speak.

Spring in the City

Right now, this morning, here
at the round kitchen table
I don't care for the moment
if it all goes.

Baroque music, like all the houses have
in movies about rich people,
is on the radio,
the plants know
about more sun coming soon

and my red mug is full of coffee.

Even outside it's the same,
the whole street for once
is doing it,
every yard on the block
is raked and sweet piles of sticks
are bundled for the trashmen—

right across from the kitchen window
another
and a big bunch of forsythia in it.

Untitled

And even the ugly child,
the fat one with the mother
who travels ever the simple
world between market and home,
never able to imagine
the upper stories
of the real downtown places

picks up the beautiful
leaf from the sidewalk
and takes a little jump
into the air. Some weather
is a gift for everyone.

1979

We're learning the beauty secrets again,
and how to dance. Mr. O'Rourke
the dancing instructor has new teeth
he's teaching Sally and Lisa to waltz.

It would all be familiar:
I spread the white cloth
on the grass and set out
the chicken, the wine, the chocolate cake.

It's all so natural, you'd recognize
your old shoes on my feet.
On this side of the river
we still have to learn

not to bleed all over the garden
to keep our heads out of ovens.

Apple Pie

On the round wood table
under the shaded lamp
a woman is making an apple pie.

It is one pie in a series
of pies she has made
and she has learned by now
to make the crust quickly.

She has passed the time
when she might have been able
to teach another how to make apple pie.
You'd have to watch carefully
to get it right, her words would leave out
most of the important details.

There has been a little snow
and it still sits in a curve
on the mullions of the kitchen window.

She's made a pyramid
of peeled apples,
the bottom crust lies draped
over the sides of the enamel pan.

One round apple in her left hand
the paring knife in the other,
she slices in, almost to the core,
turning the apple as she goes.

The apple slices are mounded
into the bottom crust. She presses
her curved right hand over them.

The left hand has sugar in it

mixed with cinnamon which she sprinkles
over the apples. She cuts
a stick of butter into small squares
and tucks them in among the apples.

She wraps the top crust around the rolling pin
and unrolls it over the top of the pie.

She flutes the edge.

All that's left is putting the pie to bake.

The children come in from the cold.
They make cats and rabbits
from the leftover pie dough.

The whole kitchen
smells of baking apples
and she touches the children,
first one, then the other,
on the shoulder.

Agnes, 1953

Wind broke the tree
in half, that storm
hurt my grandfather's house
and the garden was ruined.

But for three days in the cellar
we cooked beans over a lamp
and stayed close together

singing from the Hymnal
in our loudest voices.

The Charm

And the small golden fish
riding in the ship's dark hold
from China, from the far trade
for little sister home in Brooklyn
who was dead even as he bought
the homecoming gift

rides now in open air
around my neck, having seen light last
two lives ago and sun glints on gold
again; the unfathomable past
not in the object
but in the use we make of it.

Courage

Bars the door
against the storm
that lifts the house
only to set it down
in a new field
and she makes
the beds all smooth again.

Industry

The embroidered edge of the pillowcase,
the heel turned as the loaves rise,
your clean children, the sweet-smelling baby...

Sun streams in the garden. You lean
your hip on the open doorway, lace is growing
between your fast-moving fingers.

Grass Widow

wife to pebbles washed
up on a beach
somewhere on an island
          no one can reach with any boat
or wings   stays waiting
without seeming to wait
for anyone   spending years
becomes a beauty too fierce
for any friend or stranger
a figure
          visible from a great distance
(and the small house is hidden)
          in the clear Northern air
where even grass is cold

⋅§ VII

The Veil

Aquileia

Heavy with Latin and marble, weighed down by
heavy heavy unreal Romans: taken one day to Aquileia.
Ancient Roman port, once rival of Rome. Now only
mud, and a small museum. The old man, grinning and
bobbing, takes the tip, unlocks the heavy door. Inside:
a marble this, some marble those. But in the center a
case. In the case, scattered as though they have just
been rolled are dice. Gambling dice, made of amber;
the corners slightly rounded but the markings clear.
And in the same case a little morsel of net veil, and
scattered on the veil tiny golden flies. Houseflies
made of gold, more finely made than real ones. And I
could see the hands rolling the dice, could see the
hands that made the veil, could see the winning of it,
could see the woman waiting, and this time he returns:
bringing the veil.

Notes

The poems in Part II of the third book (Childhood, Family) are a clear instance of the interplay between the previously unpublished and the published poems. See, for instance, such poems, among others, as (in *Making the House Fall Down*) "White Tents," "The Lemon House," "Hiding"—all from the Italian phase, or rather phases, of her childhood, or "The Ship," "Moving," dealing with the return to America. Or again in *Nothing Is Lost*, "Il Marchese." There is no sure indication of dates, but certain ms. appearances cause me to surmise that the uncollected poems on these childhood-related memories post-date the published ones in most instances.

"Gold," p. 108. Compare with "Venice, 1949" in *Making the House Fall Down*.

"The Spoiled Child," p. 109. Originally the third line read, "Alone, tubercular, kept safe."

"To a Friend," p. 126. The Poem "Courage" (p. 164) is a version of this same poem—the positive obverse of it.

"Drought," p. 144. I could not find a final draft of stanza 1. Thus the stanza is my conjecture of how the various indicated changes were supposed to be organized.

"Hawkins Point," p. 137. This place in the Baltimore area, where a Black community had developed on neglected land no one else wanted, was destroyed by the dumping of hazardous wastes—at first unofficially, then (as recounted) by being chosen, above their heads, as the official site for this purpose.

"The Truth of These Warlike Women," p. 151. I have not found the source of this poem.

"Agriculture," p. 153. Hawley appears to have preferred the following version:

Agriculture

like birds scattering seeds
to plant whole forests about the world
and sit so patiently waiting
for the egg to ripen and burst

but in this instance I've used my editorial prerogative to choose what seems to me the clearer and firmer one.

About the Book

The Collected Poems of Beatrice Hawley
has been set in Trump Mediæval on the Macintosh
computer, printed on 60lb. acid-free paper by G.A. Daamen,
Inc. of West Rutland, Vermont, and bound by General
Bookbinding Co. of Agawam, Massachusetts.
Book design is by Virginia Evans.